Navigating Change

Advancing Program Management

Harold Ainsworth

Published by KDi Asia Pte Ltd

www.kdiasia.com
www.kdi-americas.com

ISBN:
978-981-11-0576-0

Table of Contents

Chapter 1:   Introduction   1
Chapter 2:   Principles of Program Management   15
Chapter 3:   Setting Up for Implementing   25
             Program Management
Chapter 4:   Tools & Techniques for Program   49
             Management
Chapter 5:   Challenges in Implementing Program   65
             Management
Resources   79

Table of Figures

Figure 1 - Example of Program of Projects to   4
           Implement Strategy
Figure 2 - Relationship between Portfolio, Programs   5
           & Projects
Figure 3 - The Performance Versus Learning Loop   6
Figure 4 - Sense Making in Program Life Cycle   16
Figure 5 - Program "Iron Triangle"   20
Figure 6 - Salience Model of Stakeholder Analysis   21
Figure 7 - Overview of the Transformational Flow   35
Figure 8 - KDIs' Change Facilitation Model   38
Figure 9 - The Triangle of Potential Disagreement   39
Figure 10 - Blueprint Process   52
Figure 11 - Assessment Matrix – Benefits Certainty   55
Figure 12 - Benefits Realization Pathways   57
Figure 13 - Simple Outcomes Diagram   58
Figure 14 - Expanded Outcomes Diagram   59
Figure 15 - Example of Systems Thinking in Practice   74

PREFACE

Audience

This thin book is aimed at senior and middle managers to provide an overview of modern Program Management, the benefits of adopting this approach, and how to implement in their organization.

The focus is on Program Management for organizational transformation rather than Program Management for operational purposes which includes improved resource utilization and capability development, although both these issues are addressed but rather in a transformation program context.

It is my hope that this book will provide managers with greater understanding and more effective approaches to implementing strategic initiatives in their organizations so these investments are more successful and deliver the planned outcomes and benefits.

Acknowledgements

Appreciation to those who have helped review material for this thin book including my colleagues Andrew Gunn, Terry Quanborough, Richard Stoneham, Genéne Kleppe, Tan Kim Leng and Dr. Nancy Harkrider.

CHAPTER 1

Introduction

"....the current accelerating rate of change and multiplicity of stakeholders make it impossible for performance-based project management to respond effectively in those situations. Effective response can only be achieved through the use of a learning loop aimed at increasing the decision maker's knowledge of the situation, as well as clearly identifying and balancing the needs and expectations of diverse stakeholders". (Thiry, 2000)

NOTE: Please note that program and programme are the same, just a different spelling between English and American English.

The Emerging Program Management Approach

The word "Program" has suffered over the years because of different definitions applied to it. For some it is simply a large project, while in the engineering and construction industry the word program is used to describe what most other people call a project schedule. Consequently you need to be very careful when using the word in that context else confusion arises. In other fields it can just simply be a loose collection of projects that may have some similar characteristics but nothing more.

There is however today a new definition emerging supported by a number of standards (see Resources) where in essence programs are a specific collection of projects which are managed and coordinated together in order to produce business benefits that would not be achieved by them individually.

I will use the definition from "Managing Successful Programmes" (UK Cabinet Office, 2011 and formerly Office of Government

Commerce or OGC).

"....a temporary, flexible organization created to coordinate, direct and oversee the implementation of a set of related projects and activities in order to deliver outcomes and benefits related to the organization's strategic objectives".

This implies that programs are designed to implement the organization's strategy, which will involve a number of individual initiatives or projects that need to be carefully coordinated in order to ensure that the business outcomes are realized.

These emerging views arise because of the historical situation where many projects were meant to achieve certain benefits but only succeeded in delivering a capability, which was not then exploited and used to deliver the outcomes and desired value to the organization.

So essentially program management is about ensuring capabilities are delivered from projects and also effectively used to achieve business outcomes and value.

Program Compared to Project Management

A very simplistic approach is to say that projects focus on delivering outputs or capabilities, whereas programs focus on delivering outcomes (and therefore benefits) from these outputs and capabilities.

Program	Project
Manages major uncertainties, complexity, ambiguity at macro level	Manages to clear objectives and deliverables at micro level and handles minor variations
Encourages learning that changes program objectives / approach	Carefully controls changes to scope
Focus on business outcomes and benefits	Focus on time, cost, quality and scope

Program	Project
Also understands that organizational change will be required to achieve outcomes	Believes that the organizational change is beyond the project scope (however the trend is to try and add this work to projects which is misguided as we will see later)
Keeps projects aligned to program and business objectives	Delivers specific project outputs

The following diagram seeks to show how a series of initiatives or projects will deliver intermediate outcomes which may have a benefit in their own right, or may simply be an enabler to achieve a final benefit. In this case the organization strategy is about reducing overall distribution costs and the various initiatives will contribute towards it but none of them by themselves will achieve this and deliver the strategy.

Program

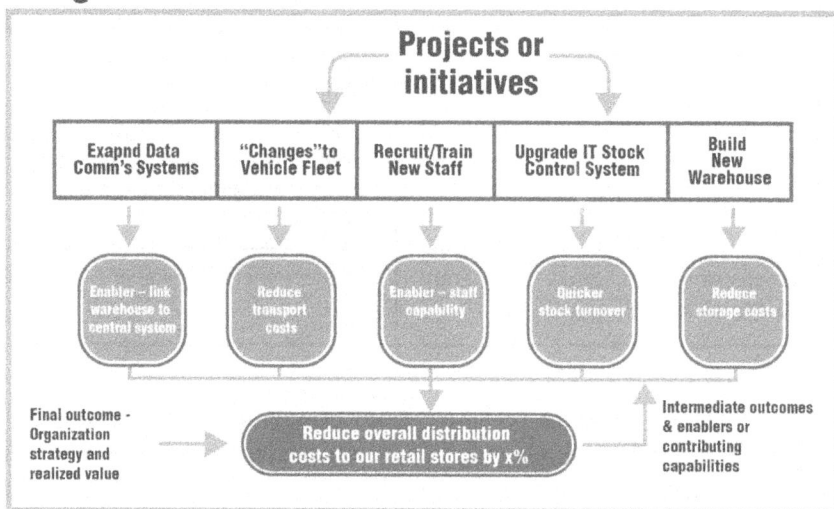

Figure 1 - Example of Program of Projects to Implement Strategy
(Example adapted from whitepaper on Benefits Management at www.pm-group.com)

This is why when implementing strategy it is useful to have a top-down approach that will coordinate the various projects which may be individually managed in various parts of the organization. In the example above IT, Human Resources, Transport and Warehouse parts of the business will each have individual projects that they will manage, but these need to be coordinated across the organization in order to achieve the strategy. If this does not happen the risk is that the strategy will not be achieved and while some individual benefits may be seen the overall benefit to the organization will not emerge.

Another view is that projects are more tactical and programs operate at a more strategic level, and we will see more of this later in reference to the skill set and level of thinking required of the program manager.

Relationship of Portfolio, Program and Project

As mentioned sometimes there is confusion around the terms portfolios and programs although less so today as the concepts are becoming more recognized. The diagram below helps to position each of these management practices and how they contribute to implementing the organization's strategy: (Thorp, 2003).

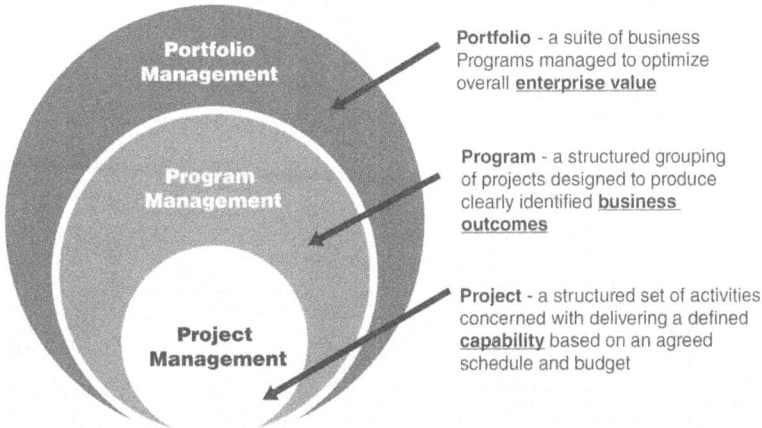

Portfolio - a suite of business Programs managed to optimize overall **enterprise value**

Program - a structured grouping of projects designed to produce clearly identified **business outcomes**

Project - a structured set of activities concerned with delivering a defined **capability** based on an agreed schedule and budget

Figure 2 - Relationship between Portfolio, Programs & Projects

Note that some projects may not be part of a program but still included in the portfolio.

Michel Thiry (2000) in the quote at start of this chapter identifies project management as a performance based activity, which is unable to deal with the complex situations we face with many strategic initiatives today. Consequently he proposes the need for a learning loop where we can make sense of the situation, seek options and evaluate them. He sees this as a value management activity which can form part of the overall program prior to the launching of specific projects, as per the diagram below from his article. As we will see later, time needs to be spent with stakeholders through workshops, interviews, discussion papers etc. to reduce ambiguity and uncertainty in the early stages of the program.

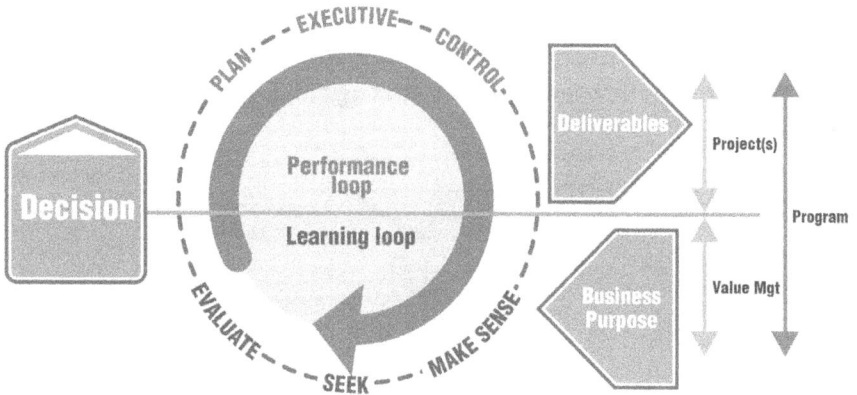

Figure 3 - The Performance versus Learning Loop

(Adapted from Thiry, 2000)

Benefits of Program Management

Research has shown and we would also know from our own corporate experience the difficulties in implementing the organization's strategy, whether it be in the public or the private sector. As we will see from this book program management is a more suitable approach to implementing strategy rather than a loose collection of separate projects driven by individual departments or divisions.

As we noted in the table above (page 2) project management has traditionally focused on delivering to scope, time, and cost (and implicitly quality) which is often called the "iron triangle" in Project Management (PM) circles, and the assumption has been that if we do this somehow the benefits will automatically flow once the capability has been delivered. There is sufficient history to show this is not the case and we cannot make such assumptions as we will see later under the subject of benefits realization. (See Chapters 3 & 4)

Therefore a program will need to consider the total scope of work required to achieve the benefits which is not just delivering the capability but also ensuring that it is embedded and effectively utilized in the organization. Depending on the particular initiative this may involve other activities such as staff training, new roles and responsibilities for certain staff or parts of the organization, new or changed processes, different ways of working, changes in the business model and even the business structure, and changed customer relationships, and even modifying the organization culture. The program will include all of these activities and ensure that they are coordinated to achieve the final outcome. There have been many examples of IT application systems being delivered which were never effectively used even though the project delivered to scope, time and cost. So it is widely recognized today that there are other factors that have to be managed to ensure ultimate success of the initiative.

To provide an illustration from the construction industry, a client may want to have a new building constructed to achieve certain ends such as reduced power consumption, reduced wastage, improved staff productivity and communications, and different ways of working (the current fashionable model is called "activity-based working" where staff do not have an assigned desk). The architect and designer will be given these desired outcomes along with the other traditional information such as facilities required, floor space etc. However in the past once the Architect and builders have finished construction and fit out they walk away from the project. For a number of years now the concept of a "post-occupancy evaluation" or POE has been promoted, the idea being that all parties involved in the project meet with the client to ascertain whether the various outputs and outcomes have been achieved. It is easier to determine the outputs such as floor space and facilities, but the outcomes such as reduced power consumption, lower maintenance costs and staff productivity etc. are much harder and longer term achievements. These POE's have not at this stage been widely used, partly because there is a cost involved in doing this work and it is a question of who should pay for it, and also I suspect because sometimes the outcomes are not achieved and we do not want to publicize that fact. I use this example to illustrate the difference between physical outputs and outcomes that deliver value to the organization.

Case Study 1: A Case Study from Construction

The following case was told to me by a student some years ago who was an Architect working for an Australian State Government education agency who had decided to implement "open classrooms" approach. Her job was to design these classrooms and build them, but she found that when the teachers moved in they were busily erecting some form of temporary dividers in the open classroom to re-create what they were used to. The forgotten part of these projects was the organizational change management of explaining the new concept to the teachers and how they could use and benefit from it, and making them feel comfortable in teaching in this new environment. In discussing this with another colleague who was a school principal, she was familiar with the idea and noted that it needed high levels of trust between the teachers in order to make it work effectively. Building this trust and understanding prior to moving into the classroom had not occurred and therefore while the physical facility was ready the teachers had not been prepared to utilize the new approach. On this basis the project had failed. What was needed was a program of work which included both the construction and also engagement with the teachers to help them make the changes in the way they operated.

Case Study 2: European Bank Case (Pellegrinelli & Murray-Webster 2011)

- In Oct 2007 – the Board approved 180 million USD program to transform the banks retail operation over 5 years, in 3 phases:
  - Build capability and showcase   2007-2008;
  - Announce new positioning   2009;
  - Refine   2010-2012.
- Expected payback within 3 years (end 2010);
- Impacts on 4,500 staff employed across 550 of own branches and 250 franchise operations;

- Aim was to restructure traditional bank branches into open, accessible environments where customers do their own transactions and get advice from staff on products and services;
- The IT platforms were very outdated, but they could not wait until they were replaced;
- The banking sector in Europe was undergoing significant change;
- The organization lacked the discipline and maturity to make such a complex change;
- The target was by 2012 to sell 50% of their products direct and generate 2/3 leads for bank staff using the Internet. New roles for staff required including a call centre operation:
  - Assembled a management team to oversee the change – called Retail Board;
  - Recruited Program Director who was part of the above Board, also ran Program Office, and led team of organizational change professionals;
  - Realized they needed to "win the hearts and minds" of the managers and staff;
  - Long weekly meetings to resolve issues and maintain momentum – continuous change and trade-offs required;
  - Strong "Governance" provided by Retail Board - committed managers who were immersed in the detail of the changes being made;
  - Program had 6 work streams each allocated to a value chain. Projects in each work stream. Business case with rigorous planning and quantitative cost-benefit analysis;
  - Funding to middle 2009 came through early benefits realization - cost reduction and revenue growth - which therefore decided the pacing of each initiative;
  - New product launched June 2007 – attracted 20,000 new customers;
  - Increased direct marketing campaigns;

- Sept 2008 GFC (Global Financial Crisis) occurred – because of the strengths of the bank they attracted 55,000 new customers;
- The conversion of branches to the new format was "industrialized" (i.e. made routine and repeatable);
- They had now exhausted the opportunity for incremental changes by patching existing systems – needed to move to low-cost straight through processing;
- Summer 2010 – transformation program had become part of life – Business as Usual (BAU) and planned changes became blurred;
- However a new bigger program emerged ("One Bank") which would absorb the Retail Bank transformation program. It included the corporate and mid corporate banking arms of the group;
- This overshadowed the plans by Retail Bank to outsource their IT or buy third-party solutions;
- Concerns that Retail Bank transformation would lose its focus and coherence - corporate banking had different focus - less customers and therefore less need for volume / standardization;
- One-Bank program executives were not as close to action and not as passionate as Retail Board - had to balance local group versus corporate needs;
- Even though the Retail Bank program was carefully planned, changes were required along the way as issues became clearer, and also evidence of success to date;
- Retail Bank program worked because there was close alignment and overlap between BAU (Business As Usual) and changes being made. Duality of Roles of Retail Board helped;
- Also the program framework that was established acted as a coordination mechanism between projects and operations,

and in the bank adopting new forms to address market challenges;

— However by early 2010 some supporters of the Retail Bank program found associated bureaucracy excessive. Originally required to ensure discipline, but now seems to be absorbing too much time and effort;

— Also some staff found they had less flexibility in new operations which was more standardized.

Some of the learnings from the case are:

• Programs can last for a long duration;

• Changes in direction can occur during the life of the program;

• Programs can involve significant organizational change;

• Programs often continue into the operational phase or merge with BAU activity as happened here;

• Changes can occur in external environment - in this case positive for them;

• They need strong Governance to be successful;

• The program was successful, at least in first stage before other bank wide events intervened;

• There can be dis-benefits which need to be carefully managed.

Variations

In my experience in Australia programs are used in government and in large corporations such as finance and telecommunications, but less so in resources and construction sectors, although the concept is certainly beginning to take hold there. The last 20 years has seen the emergence of standards for program management (see Resources), a number of textbooks, multiple training courses and the subject is often included in various master's degree programs in Universities. It is not always implemented as outlined in this book which is seeking to provide the latest thinking and practice on the topic. In some organizations there is still a degree of confusion between projects and programs but the concepts described here are being increasingly promulgated and used in more places. An area where there is possibly somewhat less application of the concept is in service type firms such as Accounting, Legal, Engineering Consultancies and Project Services firms, although some do use the concept but in a slightly amended format. Other use the word program to be loose collection of similar type projects.

The Structure of this Thin Book is as Follows:

Chapter 2 - We will discuss some of the important principles that underlie program management which make it different from project management.

Chapter 3 - A look at how we set up for implementing program management in an organization.

Chapter 4 - A review of some of the tools and techniques that might be used in program management.

Chapter 5 - Consideration of some of the challenges that organizations face in implementing program management.

Resources – References to external sources of information.

Endnotes

- Cabinet Office, UK Government (2011) *Managing Successful Programs,* The Stationery Office, Norwich
- Pellegrinelli, S & Murray-Webster, R (2011) "Multi-Paradigmatic Perspectives on a Business Transformation Program", *Project Management Journal,* Vol 42, No. 6, 4-19
- Thiry M (2000) "A Learning Loop for successful Program Management", *Proceedings of the Project Management Institute Annual Seminars & Symposium,* September 7–16, Houston, Texas, USA
- Thorp, John, (2003) *"The Information Paradox Realizing the Business Benefits of Information Technology",* McGraw Hill Ryerson, Toronto

---

CHAPTER 2

Principles of Program Management

"A key skill of good program managers has been described as 'managing the white space in between the projects', or all the activities that produce more than the sum of the parts."
(Ward et al, 2013)

Introduction

Basically my aim here is to show that Program Management is not just a larger or more complex project which it is in the minds of many people, and unfortunately including some practitioners. Program Management is seeking to achieve something different from projects, which is achieving the final outcomes and business value, rather than just building physical or other capability, such as systems, products, and services. Therefore it has different drivers and approaches and this is a very important distinction as we will discover.

The Program Environment

Because of their more strategic nature programs operate in a larger and more dynamic environment. For example an organization may have a program to launch a new product or service which can involve many activities including changes in the organization. However they are also subject to changes in the external environment, which could be due to changes by regulators, changes in the industrial relations environment, actions by competitors, and today what we are terming "digital disruption" which means that organizations are subject to new entrants with some being digitally based rather than existing traditional competitors. All of these may cause a program to change direction. The diagram below created by my colleague Richard Stoneham (web site - www.businessprocessesaustralia.com.au) seeks to show this, and while project implementation begins to take up a larger proportion of the effort over time, sense making and adaption to change continues throughout the life of the program. Ideally individual projects will only be launched when they are ready, to help minimize changes to them.

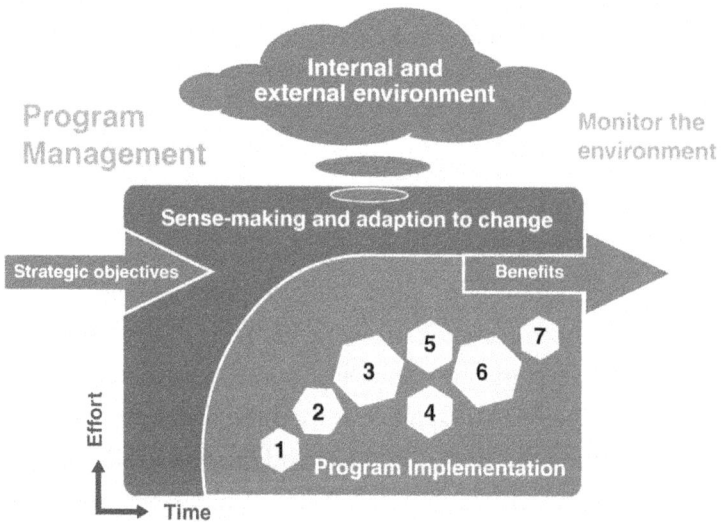

Figure 4 - Sense Making in Program Life Cycle

As noted in the quote at the start of this chapter, the role of the Program Manager is not so much focused on managing the individual project managers, who hopefully are competent to fill their role, but rather to ensure there is appropriate level of coordination between the projects, and all the subtle pieces that make up the whole are covered and some may not be specifically part of any project scope. (We sometimes use the term "ensure that nothing drops between the cracks and is lost!"). The Program Manager is also involved in scanning the environment for changes that might impact on the program.

The Focus of Program Management

As we will discuss throughout this book the focus of Program Management can be summarized as:

- Driven by the organization's strategy, it will be seeking to implement a specific strategy across the organization, and as such will be a top down approach which will coordinate the activities of a number of parts of the organization;

- It will be impacted at times from changes in both the internal and external environment, and will need to respond to these changes possibly by adapting and changing direction;

- The business case is better performed at a program level as it will take into account the contribution of various projects, some of which will produce identified benefits but many of which will be simply providing a capability (enablers) which the program will need to exploit to gain the benefits; (see Chapter 1 - Figure 1 about reducing distribution costs).

- Key focus of the program is on achieving benefits for the organization as a whole, not just individual parts of the organization, and this will require a focus going beyond scope, time and cost of individual projects;

- In order to achieve these planned benefits there will be changes required in the organization and program management will be planning and coordinating these changes, whilst not taking away responsibility from the specific business unit managers for the changes required in their area.

It should be noted that in many organizations there is a tendency sometimes because of the manager's KPIs, to focus on benefits to his/her own Business Unit rather than what is best for the organization overall. We are reminded of the quote "you cannot optimize the whole by optimizing the individual parts" (Edwards Deming and others). The focus therefore must be on optimizing for the whole organization which may create pushback from some individual business managers seeking to optimise results for their own area.

The Different Approach Required for Programs

The Decomposition pitfall - "At the heart of the project-based view is a tendency to see programs as the aggregation of the constituent projects. Consequently the program business case is the sum of the project business cases" (Sergio Pellegrinelli "Thinking and acting as a great programme manager", 2008)

As per the important quote above Pellegrinelli (2008) elaborates on the pitfalls in the "project based approach" to programs (i.e. treating them the same way). These pitfalls include:

> Definition – Which encourages organizations to strive for higher levels of program definition than warranted by the fluid program environment. Program focus needs to be on accommodating emerging requirements, exploiting opportunities and learning from experience.

> Delineation – Which may promote the purpose, internal cohesion and identity of the program as a separate entity (programs can extend for long durations) at the expense of embedding it in the fabric of the organization. (See Chapter 1 Case Study 2 - European Bank - where BAU and program activity became blurred).

> Decomposition – A tendency here to see programs as the aggregation of the constituent projects. However programs are not necessarily the sum of the component parts. (As per the quote "the whole is greater than the sum of its parts").

> ›   <u>Can-do</u> – The project level view is to do whatever is required to achieve the agreed outcomes. Programs however need to be open to radically changing the scope and outcomes depending on opportunities or changes in the internal or external environment.

> ›   <u>Enterprise wide</u> – Extension of rationality, structure and discipline throughout the organization to improve performance on projects and programs, may unintentionally stifle responsiveness, innovation and experimentation especially at a program level. Programs need to take a more flexible approach because of the strategic level issues being addressed.

Project versus Program Drivers

For project managers their key drivers is what is known in the industry as the "iron triangle" or the 3 key measures of scope, time and cost, each of which sit on the corner of one of the angles of the triangle. To be successful they need to manage these 3 components carefully, and sometimes making trade-offs between them. I would add quality which I have included in the diagram below, but some may argue that that is part of scope although I prefer to see it made more explicit since it is a different dimension of scope.

My colleague Tan Kim Leng, Founder of KDiAsia (who sponsor this series of books), has suggested that for program managers there should be a similar triangle of key drivers for the program, and he proposed strategy, change and outcomes/benefits which I would agree are very much key drivers.

Time and cost while important do not have quite the same criticality within programs and will be subservient to delivering the strategy which will deliver the benefits, subject to the appropriate changes being made in the organization.

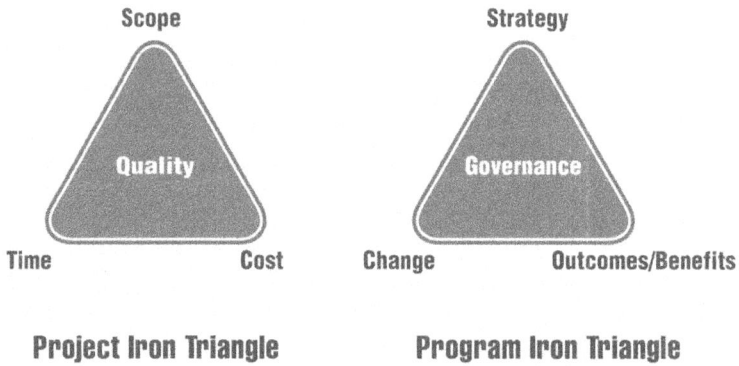

Figure 5 - Program "Iron Triangle"

So when assessing programs we should consider the "program iron triangle" drivers rather than the "project iron triangle"

Stakeholders

We know the importance of stakeholders in project management, and it is even more important at a program level since it operates at a strategic level in the organization and may involve both internal and external stakeholders. Because of this the program may be dealing with some very powerful and important stakeholders. Traditionally we have looked at stakeholders on a two-dimensional grid usually in terms of their power and interest in the project. Another model has emerged which looks at stakeholders on a three- dimensional basis, and which may be more relevant to programs. It is called the Salience model as the diagram below shows. (Mitchell et al, 1997).

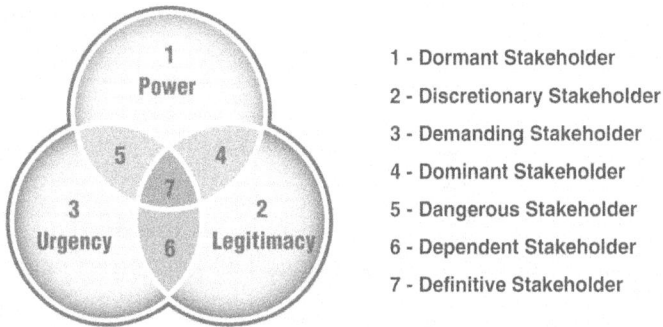

1	Power
5	4
	7
3 Urgency	6 Legitimacy 2

1 - Dormant Stakeholder
2 - Discretionary Stakeholder
3 - Demanding Stakeholder
4 - Dominant Stakeholder
5 - Dangerous Stakeholder
6 - Dependent Stakeholder
7 - Definitive Stakeholder

Figure 6 - Salience Model of Stakeholder Analysis

For the criteria above Power is obvious, Urgency relates to how quickly they expect a response to their requests, and Legitimacy relates to their authority and level of involvement.

Depending on their position based on these three criteria we can classify them as per the list from 1 to 7 – with the ideal or Definitive Stakeholder (7) being the one in the centre of the three rings.

Case Study 3: NHS IT Case (NHS = National Health Services in UK) (House of Commons, Committee of Public Accounts (2013)

Unfortunately this case does not have a happy ending, despite starting out well. It was an ambitious program designed to reform the way that the NHS uses information, and particularly moving to a paperless patient records and integrated IT systems across the NHS. The program was launched in 2002 and officially disbanded in 2011 however in 2013 the program was still operating in various forms and the final cost was still unknown as contract negotiations were being pursued with several of the supplier organizations. There were initially four large international consulting organizations involved, but at the time of the program being "closed" two of those organizations had withdrawn being owed considerable sums of money, and contract negotiations were continuing about the money claimed.

It was exceedingly complex undertaking with many stakeholders and a failure to fully engage all the stakeholders, and especially given the way the health system operates in the UK where there is considerable local regional autonomy. Therefore stakeholder engagement is absolutely critical to be successful.

There was also insufficient focus on benefits, and how they would be measured and achieved.

Initially expected to cost £12 billion the estimate at closure was around £9.8 billion but even this is uncertain as contract negotiations was still in progress. Only around £3.7 billion of benefits could be identified at this stage, and many were still be realized in the future. It was described as "not an IT software issue but a management problem" and the "worst example of value for money for the taxpayer".

Key issues that emerged were described as:

- Technology focused not business focused;

- Lack of stakeholder engagement;

- Inadequate attention to benefits realization (an afterthought);

- Failure to understand the complexity of the undertaking;

- Lack of business ownership and accountability;

- Failure to understand the extent of organizational change required.

All of these are issues that Program Management needs to address at all times.

Reflection

When working at a program level a systems view is required to understand the complexity of the situation and it is not appropriate to simply use a decomposition approach, as used with projects to break everything into its component parts. In programs mostly the whole is greater than the sum of its parts (to use a well-known quote). This implies that there are emergent properties that are not predictable which will occur, and which were not obvious when we decompose the program into its constituent parts.

The implication is that programs will need to be managed differently to projects, and will require different capabilities for program managers and governance groups and we will cover this in the next chapter.

Endnotes

- House of Commons, Committee of Public Accounts (2013) "The dismantled National Programme for IT in the NHS", *Nineteenth Report of Session 2013–14* - download from: http://www.publications.parliament.uk/pa/cm201314/cmselect/cmpubacc/294/294.pdf accessed 25 Jan 2016
- Mitchell, R., Agle, B., Wood, D: (1997) "Toward a Theory of Stakeholder Identification and Salience: Defining The Principle of Who and What Really Counts", *Academy of Management Review*, Vol. 22, No. 4, p.853-886.
- Pellegrinelli, Sergio, 2008, *"Thinking and acting like a great Programme manager"*, Palgrave MacMillan , Basingstoke, Hampshire
- Ward, John et al (2013), *"Beating the odds – the secrets of successful programmes"*, International Centre for Programme Management at Cranfield – see Resources at end for link to the paper http://www.som.cranfield.ac.uk/som/p19891/Research/Research-Centres/ICPM-Home/Publications/Whitepapers accessed 17/10/2013

CHAPTER 3

Setting Up for Implementing Program Management

"By accepting that uncertainties exist, managers can reflect more fully on the programme, both at an individual level and as part of the management team. Multiple perspectives normally exist among different programme participants, and this can lead to erroneous, if well–intentioned, decision making. The matrix technique is useful for managers to drive the necessary discussions between them so they can share their views, including significant differences of opinion and reach a consensus on their understanding of the programme and what has to be done to make it successful." (Ward & Turner, 2013)

Introduction

In this chapter we consider some of the areas that we need to address to set up for program management or to improve our approach to this practice. It will include:

- Selection of Program Managers with the appropriate skills;

- Governance of Programs;

- Program reporting;

- Program life cycle;

- Strategic level risk;

- Business cases;

- Business change management;

- Benefits realization;

- Program Management Framework.

Some organizations have endeavored to modify project management to include some of the above topics, but in my view with very limited success and which we explain why throughout this book.

Selection of Program Managers

There is a tendency to think that Program Managers will come from the ranks of Project Managers which is a natural assumption because program management used to be somewhat like project management. However as we look deeper we will see that there is a different level of thinking required at a program level. Pellegrinelli in his book "Thinking and acting as a great programme manager" (2008) clearly demonstrates this point, and shows there are a number of levels of thinking about program management as per the table below.

Level	Description
1	Programs are large complex projects, and are managed in a similar way
2	Programs are seen as more complex than project activities and need more adaptation and divergence from project activities
3	Programs are a distinct approach – focus is beneficial change in the organization

Level	Description
4	Programs have a strong future and strategic orientation • Strategy implementation • Organization development and change

Program Managers really need to be operating at level 3 and preferably level 4. We find that many Program Managers and especially those moving into the role from project management would prefer to remain at level 1 and 2 were they are more comfortable with the more clearly defined aspects, rather than working at a more strategic level where there is more ambiguity, fuzziness, uncertainty and change.

Project Managers are not always comfortable working in the environment described previously where there is change of direction, ambiguity, and often less structure and formality.

I would be reluctant to introduce a long list of potential skills that a Program Manager might need (although some writers do) and instead would suggest two very broad capabilities.

- Able to take a holistic big picture view, or what we sometimes call a systems view, understanding that there are many components that interact with each other, and that the whole is greater than the sum of the parts. Hence it is not just about decomposition into its constituent parts and reassembling it into the whole. (We deal more with the system thinking approach in Chapter 5).

- Able to understand that there is ambiguity and fuzziness and an inherent messiness in many of the situations in organizations that we are called to deal with, particularly strategy, and that there is no simple single answer. Usually it is necessary to gain the perspectives of many people in order to develop some consensus about a potential solution, and it may change over time. Programs should resolve these issues as much as possible before launching projects in order to create more certainty around delivery.

Hopefully these capabilities exist in emerging managers in the organization which means that being a Program Manager could be a useful career step for future senior managers. It also should be noted that many Project Managers would prefer to remain within the more certain and clearer domains of projects, while others would be keen to broaden their role and learn new skills in a wider Program Manager role.

Governance of Programs

Organizations have put in place structures to manage projects which may have different names such as Steering Committees, Project Boards, Project Control Group etc. Some of these operate effectively and some do not. Recently in conducting a capability assessment in a large Australian organization I found very varied (both positive and negative) feedback about the performance of such governance groups, including:

- The groups were too large to be effective (more than 10 members and some in excess of 20 or 30);

- The managers attending these meetings had no idea of their roles and responsibilities;

- Some attendees had no real stake in the project outcomes but nonetheless were very vocal;

- Sometimes effective decision-making was lacking;

- The people who were meant to attend are too busy and have delegated their responsibility to others who do not have the authority to make decisions;

- A lack of respect for the knowledge and capability of the project manager (sometimes valid but mostly not).

However some feedback from other areas of the organization about these groups was quite positive.

I want to suggest some very important principles about the Governance of Programs which I believe is more difficult than Governance of individual Projects:

- Since programs will usually cross internal organizational boundaries they must represent at a very senior-level those parts of the organization involved;

- They need to have the authority to make strategic level decisions;

- They require authority to deal with the organizational change issues, particularly where power structures in the organization can be impacted by the changes implied by the program;

- The focus of attention has to be on the creation of business value and not just delivery of capability to scope, time and cost at a project level.

Case study 4 at the end of this chapter named RTGS records where the Governance Group worked very effectively to this end.

There is no single and correct Program Organization structure but again some principles are proposed:

- An effective Program Sponsor who can make decisions, or arrange to have them made, and provides good leadership;

- A Program Manager able to take a holistic view of the various activities within the program;

- A person on the team, often called a Business Change Manager, who will coordinate those activities with the business units involved, the primary focus being on benefits realization;

- Possibly a Program Office that will look after the more administrative type matters;

- Competent Project Managers for each component project.

The organization discussed here would be reporting to a governance group for the program. Individual project steering committees may or may not be required.

Governance at a program level needs to be concerned about value so while performance reporting may cover scope, time and cost the more important aspects will be around tracking of benefits, progress with organizational change, strategic level risks, and any changes in the environment which will impact on the strategic objectives and therefore the program.

There is an increasing number of research papers pointing to the importance of effective governance in achieving business value from investments in programs and projects. Therefore governance should be given adequate attention, including the selection of suitable people to perform this role.

Program Reporting

Many programs still report as if they were a project and this is very misleading. While we want to know how the individual projects are performing (scope, time and cost etc.) the program needs to consider other more strategic factors such as:

- Are we still aligned with strategy or does the strategy need to be modified due to changes in the internal or external environment;

- Strategic level risks status (i.e. beyond delivery and technical type risks);

- Progress with outcomes and benefits – there are often intermediate outcomes that can be measured along the way;

- Progress with the business change required to achieve outcomes; (hard to measure but important)

- Continued Stakeholder commitment to the agreed original or modified vision.

It is important to have the conversation on these topics else the whole focus will simply be on deliverables which while important will not necessarily deliver outcomes which is why we are conducting the program. Of course it is easier to measure scope, time and cost and much harder to measure outcomes and benefits which explains why our current focus. As we report across the life cycle of a program the metrics we use may be different and certainly later the focus will be on whether behavior is changing to adopt the new practices, capabilities delivered etc.

In effect we need to manage the value chain at all stages by ensuring that the end value is still achievable and respond accordingly. Hence why in the table following we are checking at end of each stage to determine this, and also regularly during execution. One of my other thin books in the series Navigating Change on "Initiating Governance" suggests we need to keep this focus at all times in the life cycle to avoid slipping into a focus on outputs rather than outcomes.

Focusing on outcomes rather than deliverables is more likely to lead to changed behaviors at all levels the organization.

Concept	Business Case	Detailed Plan
Determine if the concept is worth pursuing into a full Business Case.	Sufficient information to justify proceeding with the program.	Initial design to determine final estimates. Detail on program delivery.
Is there value in proceeding to a business case stage? How long? How much?	Cost / Benefit / Risk justification to proceed. Are stakeholders committed? Can value be achieved?	Detailed plans to implement – more accurate costs and benefits. Do we still proceed?

Execution	Closure and Handover	Post Implementation Review
Execute according to the plan Make changes as required.	Handover to operations / users. Program closure. Knowledge capture.	Benefits Realization review after some period of operation.
Reporting against the plan, including cost and timeframe to complete. Do we continue? Will benefits be achieved?	Lessons Learned about delivery for future improvement.	Ensure that benefits are being achieved. Lessons Learned for future?

Program Management Lifecycle

Program Life cycles should be different from Project life cycles and several of the approaches below make this point, otherwise we can easily slip back into the project way of thinking.

Michel Thiry (2004) first outlined the approach below which was then later incorporated into his book (2010).

Phase	Activities
Formulation develop possible courses of action, determine benefits, and decide actions	• Purpose defined, understand pressure for change • Stakeholders and needs identified • Identify alternative courses of action, evaluate options and value they add • Make trade-offs and decide actions

Organization
 	
strategy planning and select best mix of actions
	Strategic level
	• Resources
	• Program team structures
	• Operational procedures
	   ○ Communication channels
	   ○ Pacing of program
	   ○ Change management
	   ○ Inter-dependencies
	
	Selection of projects:
	• Prioritization of projects;
	• Inter-dependability of projects.

Deployment execution of actions and control	Execute actions • Initiate projects • Allocate / re-allocate funds Control • Assess environment • Re-evaluation of program – "gating" process • Reassign resources

Phase	Activities
Appraisal assessment of benefits and re-pacing if required at key intervals (different to regular reporting on performance – see below)	Appraisal of: • Benefits appraisal • Threats and opportunities • Business needs / circumstances • Future of program (e.g. stop, re-pace) Conducted at two levels - program and projects
Dissolution Re-allocation	Re-allocation of people and funds and uncompleted work Knowledge management feedback

In the table above appraisal is different from regular monitoring, but rather is a planned re-assessment of the program direction in the light of changes in the internal or external environment at key stages, and also progress with achieving planned benefits. This might occur at specified intervals such as 6 months or as required when changes arise.

Programs need to continue over into BAU until the changes have become operationalized. During this time the program team are supporting the operations team through additional training, coaching, resolving issues, interpreting data and other support activities. This activity need to be carefully considered as a part of change management planning at the beginning and not as an afterthought since it can be significant effort, and failure to manage can mean outcomes will not be achieved.

In the Case Study 2 of the European Bank in Chapter 1 you will note that BAU and the program activity became blurred for a while.

The diagram below from MSP (Cabinet Office, 2011) shows that once the program is defined it goes through a number of "tranches" or phases concerned with delivering capabilities and realizing the benefits through delivery of operational capability. The idea is to break the program into a number of "tranches" each of which will build on the other. This aims at avoiding a "Big Bang" single delivery which can often be rather risky. It does take some care and thought, and often some extra cost, to break the program into a number of "tranches".

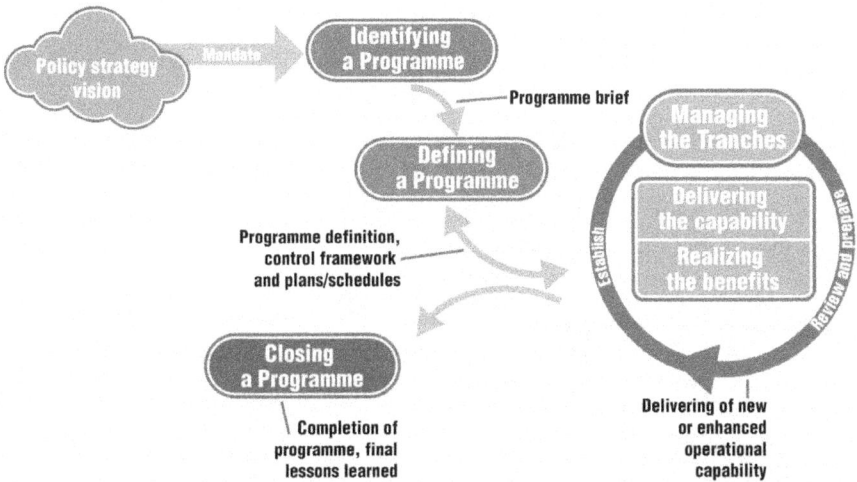

Figure 7 - Overview of the Transformational Flow
(From: "Managing Successful Programmes", 2011 The Stationery Office, London)

Strategic Risk

At a program level we begin to rise above the tactical delivery risks of a project, although some significant project risks may be escalated to a program level, and instead deal with some more strategic level risks that the program will need to consider. These may include:

— Environmental risks (legal, societal, regulatory);

— Competitive, Customer and market risks;

— Industry risks (mergers, capacity excess, etc.);

— Technology risks (external, obsolescence, etc.);

— Business partner risks (own agendas, take-over, etc.);

— Other initiatives in organization – their dependencies or impacts;

— Risks from complexity (unknowable);

— Benefits achievement (what may prevent us realizing the benefits?);

– Organization capability. (See Chapter 4 Assessment Matrices as a means of assessing this).

These risks are often harder to define and manage than those in the tactical project level, which is why it has been suggested that at this level it will require significant collaboration across the organization to both identify, understand and plan the management of these risks. It is unlikely that any single manager will be able to effectively deal with any of these strategic risks. So program risk management may need to go beyond traditional risk management as practiced in the organization in order to capture a broader view of risks and their appropriate treatment.

Business Cases

Typically business cases have been performed at a project level but it should be apparent from this book that often the real business benefits are only obtained when a number of projects are combined. This was shown in Figure 1 in chapter 1 where the strategic objective was to reduce distribution costs for retail stores through the combination of a number of initiatives. Some of these initiatives did have a value in their own right but also some of them were simply enablers or capability building.

Hence the argument is that in most situations the business case should be developed at a program level however organizations have been creating them at a project level for a long while so it does take some change of thinking for this to occur. The other challenge is that at a program level we are not going to obtain the level of detail in terms of project costs that will occur at a later stage when the project is more clearly defined. Hence for a business case for a program level we are looking at target costs and benefits which will be refined over time as additional information is obtained.

I have seen a number of instances in Australia where large corporations are looking for very definitive costs in business cases, beyond that which is feasible. These organizations mandate a plus or minus 10% variance from the actual final cost at a business case stage but it is impossible to obtain this level of accuracy until most of the design work is complete which usually occurs post business case approval. Professional estimators will confirm this view, however it is often not understood by senior management in the organization, and particularly those from a finance background who would prefer to have less variability in the cost. The result is inevitably a cost blowout. So it depends on whether you want realistic costs and are prepared to accept that cost estimates will vary depending on the level of information available resulting from the work performed on scoping and design as the program and projects proceed. This is where effective Stage Gating (review checkpoints points at end of each stage listed in tables on page 32) should stop programs or projects if their business value diminishes over time.

In my other book in the Navigating Change series "Initiating Governance" which covers Governance of Project investments we discuss in further detail the need for cost and benefit estimates to relate to the level of information available at each stage on the life cycle.

Change Management

In recent years it has become clear that one of the missing ingredients in strategic initiatives has been the need for the organization to make changes to embed and exploit the capability produced, whether that capability be a piece of infrastructure, new services or products, or enhanced knowledge or skills. Projects whether they be infrastructure or business systems based have been very good at delivering capabilities but these have not always been utilized effectively in order to gain the planned benefits. The thinking has been that once the capability has been delivered then automatically it will be used appropriately and benefits will begin to flow, and often this unrealistic assumption comes from people working on projects with a technical background.

Hence there has grown up an industry around business change management. While it is certainly helpful to have consultants and educators who can assist and guide us ultimately the business or operational manager needs to take responsibility for the changes in his or her area of the organization.

In the next chapter we mention the Blueprint as a document that will assist in understanding what the organization will look like after the program is completed, and this can help us to identify what changes are required, or as they term it "the gap" between current and future state. (See Chapter 4 – "Blueprint" for more on this).

For many organizations this means some change in the way things are done, and we know this is not easy since "it deals with the complexity of human interactions" (Harkrider and Tan, 2013). The Change Facilitation model is shown on the following page. The book and the workshops KDiAsia conducts can assist your organization in planning and adopting the necessary changes required to gain the benefits from programs implementing strategic initiatives.

People are drivers of change in an organization

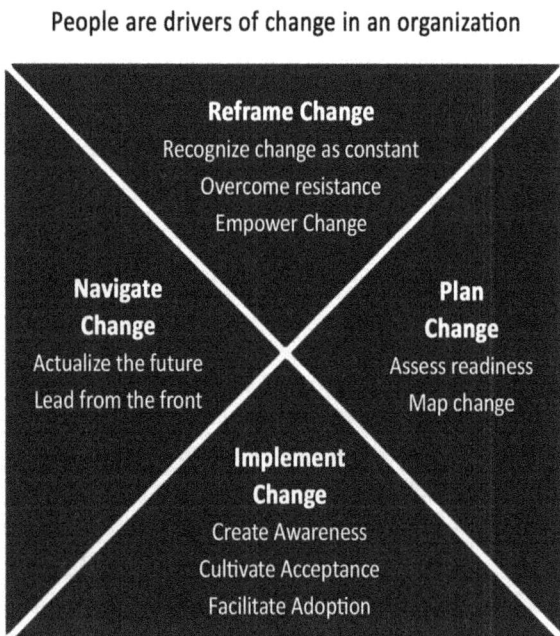

Reframe Change
Recognize change as constant
Overcome resistance
Empower Change

Navigate Change
Actualize the future
Lead from the front

Plan Change
Assess readiness
Map change

Implement Change
Create Awareness
Cultivate Acceptance
Facilitate Adoption

The leadership role changes in each phase of the model

Figure 8 – KDi's Change Facilitation Model

This KDi's Change Facilitation model above can also help to understand change through change analysis and mapping the larger change with all the smaller resultant changes as explained in Chapter 5 of their book.

One of the challenges is that in organizations there is often various perceptions at different levels about the extent of change required and how difficult it will be. The following diagram from the Cranfield Uni research is very informative about these issues (Ward et al, 2013).

They note that the Program Manager has to work with both line managers and senior executives with different perceptions about the change and also the amount of resources required (see diagram - Figure 9 - following), where the perception of line managers is that there is more effort and time required to make the changes. They suggest that there needs to be agreement between senior and line management about the scope of work before negotiating about funding and resources. Their Assessment Matrices outlined as a technique in Chapter 4 can be useful in facilitating this dialogue.

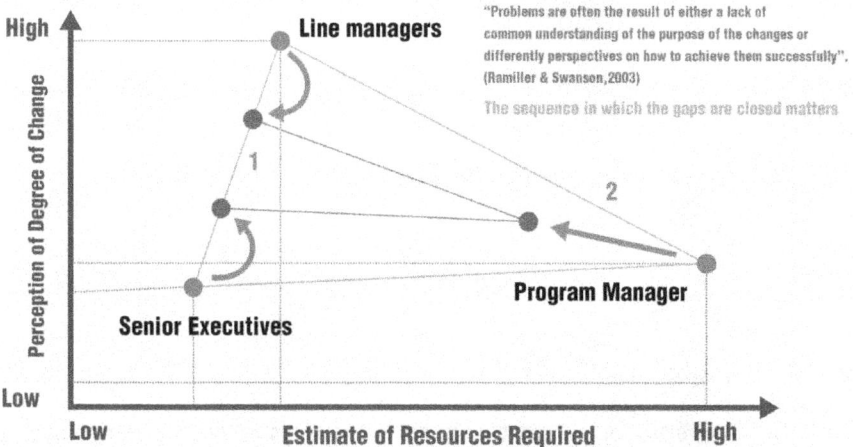

Figure 9 - The Triangle of Potential Disagreement

(From: Ward et al, 2013)

There are now many sources on the subject of change and what it involves but let me suggest a few possible areas that may be required:

- Comprehensive communications at all levels about the changes, reason for and benefits of, and future state envisaged. This need to be consistent message cascading through all levels of management from the top, to the middle and then supervisors or team leads who are close to the action;

- Changed processes and business models that are documented, tested then used appropriately to produce the planned results;

- Web sites and intranet changes, especially providing easy access to artifacts such as processes and other supporting material;

- Training and review of its effectiveness with follow up when required;

- Visible support from management in various ways and especially during the transition challenges (may include resolving quickly unforeseen issues that arise);

- Opportunities to provide feedback on the planned changes and participate in their development.

Benefits Realization

Many organizations are turning their attention today to the area of Benefits Realization but are still finding it challenging for a number of reasons:

- It requires a more robust and detailed business case including a benefits plan, which is more than just stating how much they should be and will include information on when to be realized, who is accountable, what the measures are both now and in the future, and the approach to measurement. Ultimately the program will be embedded in BAU where success or otherwise will be evaluated.

- It will require constant focus throughout the life of the program on benefits, which can be in the form of benefits realized to date, future benefits and their likelihood of being achieved, and changes to the environment which might impact on the benefits. This of course requires us to go beyond the traditional scope, time and costs that projects measure.

- Ultimately a Post – Implementation Review (PIR) will be required to see if the benefits were achieved, and also what lessons can be learned to make future improvements in the overall process. Unfortunately organizations for many reasons find this exercise difficult to implement, and one of the reasons being having resources to perform the follow-up since the program will typically have been disbanded some time before. Also because of the issue of Accountability for benefits there is a reluctance to formally document what everybody suspects, that all of the planned benefits were not achieved. There are some valuable lessons here that are not being learned if PIR's are not conducted. (Many organizations conduct Post – Project Reviews, where the emphasis is on how the project delivery performed and not on whether benefits were realized, although sometimes these reviews are also called PIR's - so the terminology can be rather confusing. PIR's should be sometime after the event, usually a six-month duration is suggested, in order to allow the capability to be embedded and benefits to appear). One of the benefits of having Process Owners for significant organizational processes is that performance measure can be attributed to the process and the Owner held Accountable. Programs can utilize such performance measures for benefits tracking – for example has any change occurred to the process measures due to the program?

Key principles of Benefits Realization (NSW Government, 2014)

1. Benefits management starts by defining the program/project objectives and the benefits they deliver.

2. Benefit identification and understanding drives refinements to the business case (as we understand more clearly what the intended benefits are, and put measure on them, it aids our understanding of the scope of work and approach required to achieve them).

3. Benefits must be aligned with the strategic goals of the organization.

4. Benefits Realization Management needs to integrate with an organization's Financial, Program, and Change Management Frameworks.

5. Benefits are enabled by successful change – people, process, technology and organizational. (E.g. benefits will not occur just because we have delivered

technology or process it need to be combined with other factors and often behavioural change).

6. Benefits need to be owned and managed by a designated person in the business; they don't just happen.

7. Benefits must be measurable and linked to performance data and reporting frameworks.

8. Benefits can be tangible (financial or nonfinancial) or intangible, e.g. improvements in quality, efficiency, access, and financial performance.

9. Benefits realization requires a baseline and benefit targets in order to measure resulting outcomes.

10. Dis-benefits need to be recognized and mitigated.

11. The same benefits cannot be claimed by two or more projects (i.e. no double counting).

12. Benefits need to be communicated.

13. Benefits are not automatically realized; active monitoring is required.

14. Benefits are dynamic; they need to be regularly reviewed and updated.

15. Intermediate outcomes are needed to realize end benefits (and are just as important).

16. Benefits tracking continues long after a program/project has ended.

Even non-financial benefits can still be quantified, for example such as levels of satisfaction by customers or users, frequency measures etc. As noted above it is important to have intermediate outcome measures, which we will deal with in the next chapter, as these provide a means of checking progress towards end benefits. The end benefits may take some time to be realized, even years, so intermediate measures are extremely important in these cases. Also for certain types of benefits we may want to measure the short-term and the long-term, for example the launch of a new product or service may generate a very positive initial response from customers, but we will want to understand whether that response can be sustained over a longer period of time after the initial novelty has worn off.

Program Management Framework

It will be necessary to set up a framework for managing programs which recognizes that it is not the same as project management including a different life cycle as mentioned earlier in this chapter. The Framework will also include roles and responsibilities, reference to the governance structures, and some templates for key documents. It should be noted that today for project management there are very well defined frameworks, methods, templates, checklists and procedures in abundance that you can select from. However in the area of program management it is not as mature and it will be different in each organization since it operates at a more strategic level. While the OGC Managing Successful Programmes approach has lots of suggestions about program management documents, my advice would be to be selective here, and define what is appropriate to the type of programs that your organization will be conducting. The principles outlined in Chapter 1 and 2 will guide you in establishing an appropriate type of Program Management Framework for your organization. You may need to start with a more basic framework and develop over time as experience is gained with the program management approach.

Some basic material that you will need includes:

- Program Life cycle explained – with sufficient time up front to make sense before launching into execution;

- Tools to facilitate program planning – such as Blueprint, Outcome maps (or Value or Benefit maps), for understanding the problem - see Chapter 4, or Value Engineering to find a better solution to deliver same or more value at lower cost;

- Program Plan – which may include high level roadmap or network type diagram, risk, stakeholders, quality, reporting, organization and roles and responsibilities;

- Change Management Plan; (the detail will differ for each program);

- Benefits Register / Plan and associated supporting documents (some of these metrics in a benefits register may overlap with or be included in organizational KPI's);

- Business Case suitable for the level of detail available for a program;

Quality Management

There is a tendency in program management to see quality management as simply an escalation of quality management on the individual projects. Whilst it is acknowledged that at a program level we will want to know that the individual projects are managing quality appropriately that is not the total picture, and Managing Successful Programmes (Cabinet Office, 2011) takes a broader view. It proposes that at a program level we need to ensure that the right stakeholders are still involved and committed, the blueprint or "end-state vision" is still relevant, and management procedures are in place to see that the end objectives and benefits of the program can still be achieved. Also that all of the above is still aligned to the organization strategy and the environment has not changed and made it no longer relevant.

Case Study 4: RTGS Case

A major Australian bank was a participant in an inter-bank program to establish an intra-day payments clearing system, which also involved for this bank significant replacement of internal legacy payment systems including a new application package from overseas. A Governance forum consisting of very senior executives who reported to the CEO was established, and several external consultants engaged. Any roadblocks were quickly cleared. There were other stakeholder forums at a more operational level to resolve detailed issues.

A Program was established with a business focused Program Director and a number of projects and with several external experienced project managers engaged. The Program Director was a business executive and not a Project Manager. He recruited a very experienced Project Manager to run a Program Office and an experienced change manager / project manager to be responsible for the business changes required.

The project involved considerable organizational change, and also the management of an overseas based software supplier, and coordination of changes to internal existing IT application systems.

The Program was successful and regarded as one of the most effective initiatives in the Bank for some years. This was attributed to sound governance, a program approach that focused on the business change required, good Sponsorship, and adequate advice on the business issues from external IT consultants who also had significant experience in the business domain.

Reflection

To set up programs it is not just a case of having a framework or methodology and other important aspects will be recognizing a different life cycle for programs, and identifying the appropriate people to be program managers. Also setting up effective governance for programs and ensuring that the program operates across organizations silos will be an important component. It will also be necessary to look at some of the practices in the organizations such as business cases and where they are best prepared, and the strategic nature of risk on programs may require a different approach. Also review the organization's capability to undertake the business changes implied by the implementation of strategies through a program needs assessment. (See Chapter 4 - Assessment matrices)

Endnotes

- Cabinet Office, UK Government (2011) *Managing Successful Programs,* The Stationery Office, Norwich
- Harkrider, Nancy & Tan, Kim Leng (2013) *Leading Change that Matters – Making Adoption a Reality*, KDi Asia, Singapore
- NSW Government, (2014) Benefits Realization Management framework – Part 1 Principles, June - available from; https://www.finance.nsw.gov.au/publication-and-resources/benefits-realisation-management-framework

- Pellegrinelli, Sergio, (2008), *"Thinking and acting like a great Programme manager",* Palgrave MacMillan , Basingstoke, Hampshire,
- Thiry, Michel (2004), "FOrDAD, a programme management life-cycle process", *International Journal of Project Management,* issue 22, pages 245-252
- Thiry, Michel (2010) Program Management. Gower, Farnham, UK
- Ward, John et al (2013), *"Beating the odds – the secrets of successful programmes",* International Centre for Programme Management at Cranfield – see Resources at end for link to the paper
- Ward, John and Turner, Neil (2013) *"Programme Assessment Matrices",* International Centre for Programme Management at Cranfield – see Resources at end for link to the paper

CHAPTER 4

Tools & Techniques for Program Management

Systems thinking is a discipline for seeing wholes. It is a framework for seeing interrelationships rather than things, for seeing "patterns of change" rather than static "snapshots" (Peter Senge, Author of The Fifth Discipline, 1990 and other works.)

Purpose of Tools and Techniques in Program Management

The purpose here is not about decomposition to better understand the problem as we would do with Project Management, but rather *sense making* in order to better understand the environment and the total system that we are working with in. As such there is a recognition that it may change over time and it will be necessary to live with a degree of ambiguity. While key stakeholders may all appear to be in agreement the reality is that there may be different interpretations placed on some aspects of the program by various parties. Some of this may not emerge until later. The tools and techniques listed below are meant to assist in the *"sense making"* process.

Why We Need Another View

When we take a systems view the cause-and-effect of various actions will not be as obvious as we desire and therefore it will be difficult to predict outcomes with certainty.

Dörner (1996) notes that "We do not neglect the implicit problems of a situation because thinking about the possible side effects of the measures we are planning would overburden us terribly. Rather, we neglect them because we do not have those problems at the moment and therefore are not suffering from their ill effects. <u>In short we are captives of the moment</u>". In other words we do not think about problems we do not have and this limits our ability to understand the totality of the situation, and the side effects that might emerge as a result of our actions. I believe this explains why certain actions taken by both governments and organizations, and even individuals, produce what we then call "unintended consequences", and there are many examples of this. These are not the planned consequences of our action but happen because we do not understand the totality of the situation and cannot envisage unforeseen impacts emerging.

Dörner's book is fascinating reading since it explains our limitations in dealing with complex situations for a number of reason including the above. Other areas include:

- Delayed feedback, (i.e. lack of immediate results from our actions) leading to confusion if it does not occur when we expect it. Often there is an inherent delay in receiving feedback which we need to allow for;

- Goals that contradict because they are not clear and we cannot adequately prioritize;

- Trying to optimize every part of the system which is impossible to do at the same time as optimizing the whole system. In a system we need to make trade-offs between various priorities (e.g. in an organization sometimes an individual department or division cannot optimise their component and must defer to what is good for the whole organization);

- Our assumption that change is static when the rate can both grow and grow quickly.

Strategy is often quite complex as it involves many factors that have to be understood and balanced, which is why the programs that implement it needs careful consideration both at the start and during the program, and a program manager who is able to see both the whole, and the patterns of change occurring.

Blueprint or "End-state Vision"

Managing Successful Programmes (MSP) (Cabinet Office, 2011) places considerable emphasis on the idea of a Blueprint or "end-state vision" as a document guiding the program. It outlines how this document should be created and what it should contain. It is important artifact that seeks to ensure stakeholder agreement and a clear picture of what the situation will look like after the program is completed. Another name for it is "target operating model" and it is described using the terms in the following table:

The POTI model – potential scope of Blueprint	
P	Processes, business models of operations and functions including operational costs and performance levels
O	Organization structures, staffing levels, roles, skills, requirements, organizational culture, supply chain and style
T	Technology, buildings, IT systems and tools, equipment, machinery and accommodation
I	Information and data required for the future business operations and performance measurement

The process and role of the Blueprint (Cabinet Office, 2011) is outlined in the following diagram.

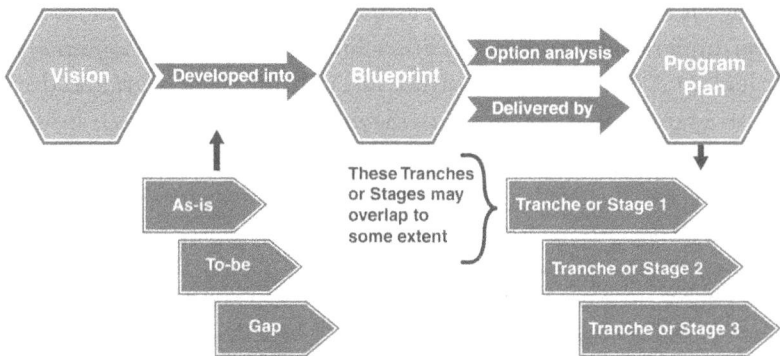

Figure 10 - Blueprint Process

Tranches are the words MSP uses for partial delivery components and benefits over time. The blueprint is developed from an "as is" state into a "to be" state with an understanding of the "gap" between the two.

The Blueprint is an important stakeholder communications document and should be reviewed from time to time to ensure that it is still current as the internal and external environment can change during the program. It is not easy to develop the Blueprint as we need to have the right stakeholders involved in creating it and this will take time and effort on the part of knowledgeable and otherwise busy people. The Blueprint because it describes the future state can also assist in determining the organizational changes required to deliver it. It can take various forms including narrative, tables, pictures and diagrams.

Selected Tools and Techniques

The following table lists some of the potential techniques that may be used in program management and their purpose, and in some cases references to relevant source material.

Technique	Purpose
Facilitated workshops	Create dialogue and gain consensus

Technique	Purpose
Benefits Maps (see note below)	Create dialogue on how outcomes are to be achieved
CSF's - Critical Success Factors (Thiry, 2010)	Provide more defined outcome measures
Achievability matrix (Thiry, 2010)	Understand challenges & risks of the program
Assessment Matrices (Ward, John et al., 2013) (see note below)	To facilitate conversation about various aspects of the program including capacity, capability, benefits certainty etc.
Scenarios Analysis	Consider and test a range of future possible options & outcomes
Options analysis	Evaluate solution options using agreed relevant criteria
Stakeholder analysis	Analyze stakeholder needs and inputs and concerns
Functional analysis	Value of specific functions in a solution – what contributes most value
SWOT analysis (strengths, weaknesses, opportunities and threats)	Understand area to focus on
Root cause analysis	Ishikawa diagrams are one version (also known as Fishbone diagrams). Other versions are Current Reality Tree from Theory of Constraints (Dettmer, 1998) which is a more detailed and dynamic approach
Modelling techniques e.g. SSM (soft systems methodology)	Understand how components combine to create possible solution. Uses Rich Pictures to create understanding of the players and issues involved.

Technique	Purpose
Gap analysis between "as is" and "to be" states	Understand the potential scope of work

There is of course the whole organizational change management issue in order to assist the implementation, but it has not been included above as dealt with elsewhere, and most of the topics above are more about creating initial understanding of scope and outcomes.

Assessment Matrices (Cranfield) (Ward et al, 2013)

These matrices were developed as a result of a research by the Cranfield University into program management across Europe, and they are designed to facilitate dialogue among stakeholders during program startup. They cover 5 topic areas:

- Benefits certainty - How much is known about the benefits and the changes required to achieve them?

- Approach certainty – What are our levels of knowledge and experience of the methods and approaches that are appropriate for the types of changes involved?

- Capability availability – Does the organization or other parties have proven capabilities to apply methods and approach to the changes needed by the programme?

- Capacity availability – Are the resources available for the programme when required?

- Internal supply: capability and capacity – What resources can be supplied by the organization, and what is the nature of the Program's control over them?

54

Also there is another matrix used later covering Deployment and Operational readiness - *Assess issues likely to affect deployment effectiveness and benefits delivery.*

An example of one matrix *(Ward et al, 2013)* follows on the next page:

Benefits certainty

		Low	Medium	High	
Nature of change	**Technology**	Technology based benefits are not established, ambiguous, not agreed and/or likely to change considerably.	Benefits resulting from the technology changes are incomplete or partially ambiguous and it is not clear how some could be measured.	Technology based benefits are fully established, evidence-based, measurable, entirely agreed and/or stable.	**How much is known about the benefits and changes required to achieve them**
	Business	Benefits of changes to business model or processes are not established, ambiguous, not agreed and changes to achieve them are not clear.	The benefits of business model or process changes are incompletely established or agreed, or are not yet entirely clear.	The business model and process benefits and changes required are fully defined and agreed.	
	People	The social or organizational impact is not understood or ambiguous, and neither the benefits nor changes are agreed.	The social or organizational impact is partly established, but uncertain in some aspects or some changes are not yet acceptable or agreed by some stakeholders.	The social or organizational benefits nor changes are fully understood, clearly defined and agreed by stakeholders.	

Figure 11 - Assessment Matrix – Benefits Certainty

After discussion one cell of the matrix is selected for each row – and it can be colored green, amber or red as is most appropriate. The point is to identify strengths and weaknesses in the program during start up so that suitable action can be instituted to resolve any areas of weakness, or at least to recognize them and monitor them for further action throughout the program. These matrices are a useful way of facilitating conversation among stakeholders before the program is launched. It is not a "tick the box exercise" but rather one of creating dialogue.

Benefits Maps

In order to deliver the outcomes the program must understand what initiatives or projects need to be launched, how they are connected to each other, and how when combined with relevant organizational change they will bring about the final outcomes and benefits. The idea is to move away from a simple cause-and-effect model that says if we implement X then we will obtain result Y, since there are many instances where this has proven to be untrue. This particularly occurs with IT application systems which simply provide the capability but do not by themselves produce the desired business outcomes. Customer Relationship Management Systems are classic example of this, where considerable money has been spent implementing computer software applications (capability) without obtaining the desired business results. The computer application system is a small part of a significant organizational change required to obtain the benefits. The other very significant activities required include an understanding of the customer relationship both current and desired, the products and services the organization offers and how these impact on the customer relationship, the organizational processes and the staff capability and capacity to deliver the necessary products and services. This is explained well in Ray McKenzie's excellent book (McKenzie, 2001) on the subject.

There are a number of possible diagramming and mapping techniques that are available such as:

- Strategy Maps (Kaplan and Norton, 2004);

- Benefits Dependencies Network (Ward et al , 2004);

- Results Chain (Thorp, 2003).

There are numerous other techniques available and some of which have been derived from the above.

The philosophy behind these mapping techniques is shown in the diagram following from Managing Successful Programs (Cabinet Office, 2011).

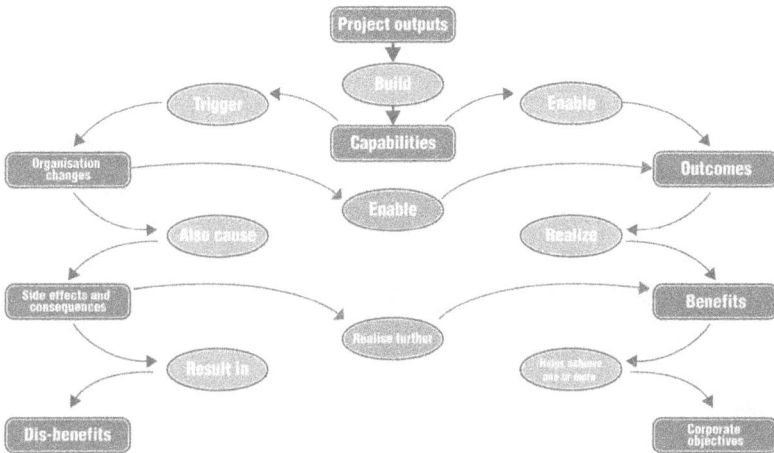

Figure 12 - Benefits Realization Pathways

The work of the program is to manage the projects which build the capabilities and then to coordinate all the other activities such as organization changes, realizing benefits and managing side effects and consequences. All of this is why program management, as it ties all these pieces together, is more difficult than project management which is delivering a more defined capability.

At a program level understanding the connections between various actions or projects and outcomes is very important, for ensuring a full understanding of the scope of work, the underlying assumptions, and the amount of business change required. Often in their minds executives will have a more simplistic view until such time as this has been appropriately mapped and discussed, when it will become obvious that the scope of work is larger. In the simple example below (based on the Results Chain approach, (Thorp, 2003)) a number of actions will lead to improved projects, including establishing a PMO (Program Management Office), improving the method and training the PM's.

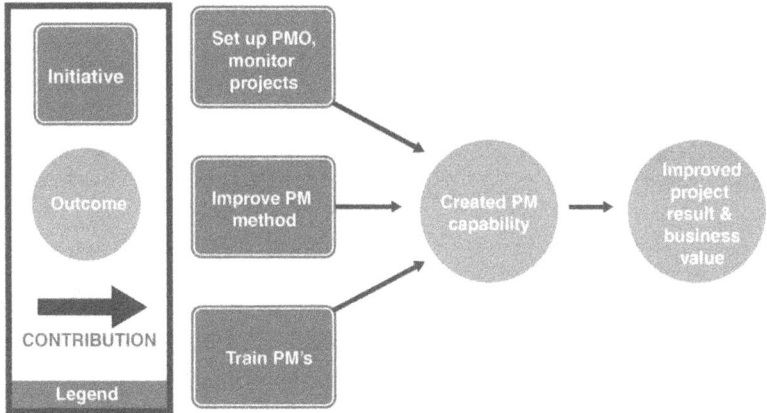

Figure 13 - Simple Outcomes Diagram

However the above simplistic map only requires a brief discussion among relevant stakeholders to understand that the view is not realistic and increased PM capability will not lead to improved results. A more complete picture would be more like this following diagram on next page, depending on the circumstances.

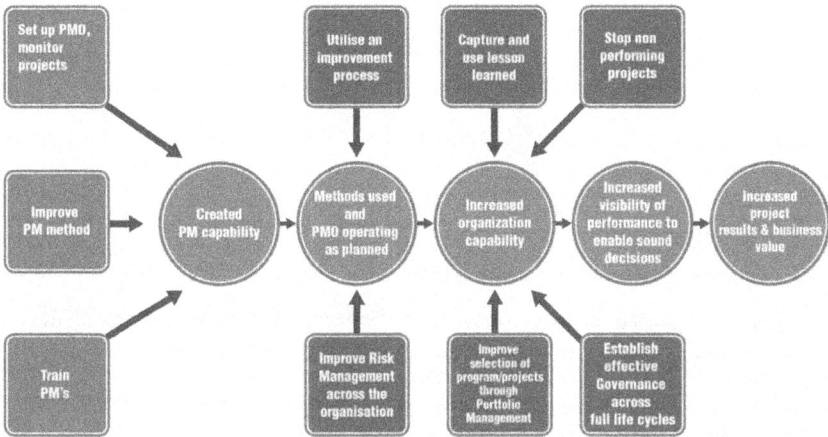

Figure 14 - Expanded Outcomes Diagram

In the above diagram there are additional activities that need to be managed such as making improvements and utilizing lessons learned as well as the important contribution of Governance is acknowledged. If the Governance groups are not appropriately established as mentioned earlier in Chapter 3 and do not operate effectively, then it is unlikely that the improved project results and the business value will be achieved. So the program will need to give attention to these other contributions some of which may involve organizational change. The issue here is one of ensuring the sufficiency of the cause and effect, and that we are not presuming that a single or a few initiatives will be the only contribution to create the desired end result. It also assists in development of plans and blueprints and in identifying key initiatives, their sequencing and dependencies.

There is often a tendency for the reaction to these detailed maps to be "this looks complex", (the one just described is simple in order to illustrate the point) and often this is the nature of the program undertaking so we should not be surprised. They will ask for more high level maps which is possible, but they will also disguise the complexity and may lead to lack of appropriate response. Also at a more detail level it will be possible to link managers KPIs to achieving specific outcomes, which is highly desirable.

Timelines

Most projects will use a scheduling tool (e.g. MS Project, P6 etc.) to list all the detailed activities, their dependencies, resource allocation and duration, however at a program level we need a much higher level roadmap that shows the individual projects, key interdependencies between them and focusing on change management activities, which could be operated as a project within the program. Also particularly we need to include the handover into operations which can carry on for some time, as typically with projects there is a defined handover point but with programs they will sometimes continue into the operational phase for a period until settled. Some of the program team may even transition into the ongoing operational group. The program roadmap will also include some of the early upfront activities prior to launching the individual projects. Personally I prefer not to use scheduling tool for this roadmap as it implies a level of detail or precision that does not exist, at least initially.

In a program the dependencies can be challenging since there are often a number of business units in the organization contributing to the overall program who understand their contribution, but may not fully understand the contribution of other business units, the potential for overlap and the interdependencies. For a project these are typically mapped in a detailed project schedule, at a program level the subtleties involved and the independence of the business units make it much more challenging. One approach is to utilize the Blueprint suggested above, and then have the relevant teams across the business units exchange information about their activities, in a facilitated workshop, so that any interdependencies can be highlighted.

The Challenges with These Tools & Techniques

The challenge with utilizing the tools and techniques described above is that they are likely to appear less conclusive, and will possibly open up the issue more rather than close it down. (That is initially create more divergence of opinion rather than convergence and agreement) This is all part of sense-making or learning loops that Michel Thiry mentioned and we covered in Chapter 1 Introduction. Managers responsible for delivery may not be comfortable with this situation since they want to start implementing the "solution" even if not fully clarified. Of course it is possible to be conclusive and converge on a solution which will be suitable for part of the program, however there may be other parts of the program where this will not be feasible. This situation should be acceptable and plans made to investigate further into that uncertain part of the program with the aim at a later date of reaching a conclusion about that specific component.

Case Study 5 - A Government Agency Undergoing Transformation

The agency was going through significant change over a multiyear period and receiving special government funding in order to achieve the stated goals. There were number of projects or programs in various parts of the organization but the division I assisted for a while had a program consisting of number of specific projects covering process change, changes to ICT systems, development of better management reporting from the ICT system, new structures being established with different responsibilities, public websites being enhanced to provide more information and guides to users, better coordination with other government agencies who needed to be consulted, and some basic level of training for staff. The program was actually being run as a large project.

There was no change management plan as the assumption was that staff would quickly adopt whatever was developed which was certainly not the case and there was some resistance and some lack of understanding by many staff of the overall purpose and approach being adopted. Most of the focus was on producing deliverables even though there were some specific outcomes they were required to achieve which were tied to the special funding they were receiving.

A number of actions were taken to improve the situation including a change readiness assessment by an external consulting organization, the development of a change management plan to ensure that the changes were adopted going forward, development of some outcome maps to explain how the various work streams fitted together to produce the outcomes, and a focus on performance reporting on outcomes and progress with change not just deliverables. We also reestablished a governance forum which had been disbanded almost a year before, to provide a forum for discussion especially on change issues, collaboration and obtaining direction and decision from senior executive management. Some reallocation of work streams among senior managers occurred in order to provide better oversight.

Leadership at the top of the division also needed to be improved. In discussions with other consultants I discovered the situation here was similar to other government agencies where significant change was occurring. Even though there was excellent material available from the government website on benefits realization and managing programs and change but it was not being utilized very widely. While there was considerable pressure from Treasury to focus on outcomes in the agencies, their management was still finding this difficult to implement.

Earlier in this chapter I briefly discussed a book by Dörner (1996) on The Logic of Failure and in the next chapter 5 I talk about systems thinking which is related to this book. I believe that ensuring we focus on outcomes requires us to see the whole system and it interrelated parts not just the individual components. It will also help to drive organizational change by focusing on desired outcomes.

Reflection

The tools described here may not be "hard" tools (definitive and quantitative) but rather "soft" qualitative techniques used to engage the various stakeholders to endeavor to reach consensus about the outcomes required and the initiatives and changes that will need to be implemented. Initially there may be some degree of disagreement but we expect that over time as we gain a better understanding and as assumptions are surfaced we will converge on both the approach and solution. The principle here is to spend more time at the start to develop as much consensus as feasible before we launch, so that we have a sound basis to work from otherwise we end up with considerable re-work later.

Endnotes

- Cabinet Office, UK Government (2011) *Managing Successful Programs,* The Stationery Office, Norwich
- Dettmer, H W (1998) *Breaking the Constraints to World-Class Performance,* ASQ Quality Press, Wisconsin
- Dörner, Dietrich (1996). *"The Logic of Failure – recognising and avoiding error in complex situations",* Basic books, New York
- Kaplan, Robert S, & Norton David P, (2004), *Strategy Maps - Converting intangible assets intangible outcomes,* Harvard Business School, Boston

- McKenzie, Ray (2001) *The Relationship Based Enterprise – Powering Business Success through Customer Relationship Management*, McGraw-Hill Ryerson, Toronto
- Senge, Peter (1990) *The Fifth Discipline*, Random House, New York
- Thiry, Michel (2010) *Program Management*, Gower ,Farnham Surrey
- Thorp, John, (2003) *"The Information Paradox Realizing the Business Benefits of Information Technology"*, McGraw Hill Ryerson, Toronto
- Ward, John, Murray, Peter, & Daniel, Elizabeth, (2004), *Benefits Management Best Practice Guidelines*, IS Research Centre, School of Management, Cranfield University
- Ward, John et al (2013), *"Beating the odds – the secrets of successful programmes"*, International Centre for Programme Management at Cranfield – see Resources at end for link to the paper

CHAPTER 5

Challenges in Implementing Program Management

"Unless we start our investigations of complex problems with a "clear recognition" of their "messiness", that is, their inherent ambiguity and uncertainty, then we seem destined to misperceive the exact nature of the problem." (Mitroff & Lindstone, 1993)

Introduction

There will be challenges in implementing program management or adapting our current version to the current good practice thinking on the topic as promoted in this thin book. These challenges include:

- Seeing it as just another overhead;

- Believing project management can be modified to suit;

- Failure to understand that it requires a change of mindset and focus particularly around outcomes and value;

- Locating suitable Program Managers and Sponsors;

- Since programs are often across organizational boundaries both internal and external they need to be coordinated at the highest level;

- The need to take a holistic view and adopt systems thinking (the whole is greater than the sum of its parts) and not be misled by simple decomposition models.

Another Overhead

Program Management can be seen as just another overhead and not required as we already have project management which is performing the same activity. This view arises because people do not understand the significant difference, as well as the challenges in actually achieving the planned value from implementing strategy and other initiatives in the organization. At the time of approving the business case it all looks simple and the value achievable but as we all know from experience it is actually a lot harder than it appears in the business case document. When the value is not achieved it can becomes a blame game but that is not helpful since we really need to understand what is wrong with the system for planning and delivering business value.

Modifying Project Management

While there has been considerable recognition in various places of the limitations of project management in achieving business value rather than just outputs, unfortunately the solution of some researchers, writers, teachers and practitioners has been to attempt to modify project management to achieve the same ends as program management. Personally I find this approach very misguided for a number of reasons. I have worked with and taught literally thousands of project managers in my career. I find the mindset between project managers and program managers significantly different. The skill sets required as noted earlier are also quite distinctive, therefore it seems to me rather challenging to find people who can achieve both the outputs and the outcomes. You can end up with a lack of focus about what you are going to achieve. Project management when practiced professionally with the right project manager and team can be very successful as I know personally from working in a project services company in the 80s and 90s. If it is working well why change it when there is another approach called program management designed to achieve other objectives. I suspect that some of the people wanting to modify project management have never seen both very professional project management and very good program management operating effectively and therefore do not fully appreciate the difference.

Once you begin to fully understand the purpose and focus of program management, the different requirements of a program manager and the tools and techniques you would not try to combine them with sound professional project management. The quote at the start of Chapter 1 by Thiry about performance based project management and the need for sense making by programs, is still very relevant here.

Change of Mindset

As discussed earlier program management requires a different mindset operating at a strategic level with a focus on outcomes and value which means that all those involved in the program, including the Program Manager, Sponsor, and Governance group (by whatever name it is called), all need to think differently and clearly about business value and how it will be achieved. This is a lot harder than thinking about scope, time, quality and cost. They also will need to understand that the program may need to change in response to changes in the environment, which is the reason we try to keep projects short and focused to avoid too many changes to them. Making changes to a program is not an approach that some managers are comfortable with especially if the organizational focus is on scope, time and cost as for projects, but change might be required in order to achieve outcomes which is a much more important criteria. Changes in programs can occur due to changes in legislation or regulations, competitor's actions, market dynamics, technology disruption, change in the focus of the organization due to movements at Board or CEO level, industry level changes, failure to be able to launch in a timely manner, increasing risk etc. There is no point continuing with a program when circumstances change and value cannot be delivered so a new direction is indicated and needs to be thoughtfully considered.

While it may seem strange to talk about the need to focus on value, since you would expect all managers in the organization to be doing this, we need to recognize that value has different meanings depending on where you might be located in the organization. For some it is more about cost cutting and for others it may be more about building capability so value is contextual as per the table below.

Who	Financial	Non-financial	Other
CEO / Board	Share price or budget / funding in Government agencies	Stakeholder value Achieve strategic objectives	Manage Risk, Survival
CFO	ROI	Resource efficiency	New innovations
CIO	Reduce IT costs	Align with business objectives	Partner with and enable the business
COO or Business Managers	More revenue and / or less costs	Efficiency – more productive, improve service levels Support achievement of KPI's	Build a sustainable capability

There has also been discussion in recent years about the need to take a long-term sustainable focus for business value, and not just a short-term focus, often quarterly, particularly for those public organizations listed on the stock exchange and concerned about their share price value. To keep the share price level they may need to take short-term decisions to satisfy the market. Some CEOs and boards have been pushing back on this in recent times and suggesting it is not sustainable and not desirable to do this and that investors should be looking at the longer term and not whether the share price has gone up or down in the last month.

The Challenge with Outcomes

As we have discussed in this book measuring outcomes is difficult and it is often easier to revert to measuring those things that we know and understand better, particularly time and cost.

"Programme performance measurement is problematic, especially measuring progress and achievement in relation to the business strategy and programme objectives and benefits. ....The aspects that need to be managed and therefore measured will evolve over the lifecycle of the program and what is measured at each stage will influence behaviors. Some measures therefore are to create or encourage the future behaviors required, rather than measure progress" (Ward et al, 2013)

As we can see from the above quote based on research findings from 21 case study programs, establishing appropriate program measures is very challenging even for experienced organizations. It will require a level of maturity on the part of stakeholders, governance groups and program managers to both identify and utilize appropriate measures. In my own experience it is best to start to use some simple, easy to implement measures and if they are not suitable discard and find other measures, rather than keep looking for the perfect measure and never settling on anything.

As we noted under benefits realization earlier, there needs to be interim measures, some of these will be actually measuring changes in behavior as suggested in the quote above.

Linking program measures to existing organizational measures can be helpful although some of these measures may be too focused on individual departments or divisions rather than the overall health of the organization which will limit their usefulness. What programs ultimately need to measure is the change implied by the program intervention.

Locating Suitable Program Managers and Sponsors

We have mentioned earlier the mindset and skill set required of Program Managers and obviously their Sponsors, and it will not be easy to locate enough of these people. Sometimes they will already be in other management roles.

Some years ago I undertook a capability study for a large Australian organization which sourced Program Managers from the ranks of middle management for the duration of the program. This was an excellent approach since the recruited Program Manager had already proved themselves adept at management at a business level the only challenge was that after they have several years as a Program Manager, they are often been bypassed by their peers for promotion, despite the unique experience gained as a Program Manager. So the idea was great except the execution of it was disconnected from the rest of the organization's career development plans.

So undertaking a role as a Program Manager for the duration of a program should be seen as a career enhancing move for the manager. It will develop their understanding of the overall business since mostly programs will be across organizational silos, and they will need to take a systems view of the many contributing factors that will lead to the success of the program.

The downside will be that they will need to interact with powerful stakeholders controlling various functions within the organization who may or may not be supportive of the program. Hence they will need a powerful and active sponsor at the top of the organization who will ensure that all the functional units support the program through aligning the KPIs of the business unit managers involved to the outcomes of the program.

Cross Functional Programs

Following on from the above this is why strategy should be a top-down approach in the organization so that individual business units are not seeking to implement strategy without overall coordination.

Unfortunately in many organizations the strategy is fairly high level and individual business units propose projects to fulfill part of the strategy, but these individual projects are not coordinated and aligned often resulting in competition rather than collaboration.

Sull et al (2015) report from their survey into strategy execution "whereas companies have effective processes for cascading goals downward in the organization, their systems for managing horizontal performance commitments lack teeth.....More than half (of the managers surveyed) want more structure in the processes to coordinate activities across units". Lack of collaboration across business units creates significant problems for programs.

Case Study 6 – "Room for the River" (from Rijke, et al, 2014)

The aim of this paper is to explore how program management can contribute to the effective design and delivery of megaprojects. The paper focuses on program design and interactions between the management of individual projects and the program as a whole. The case study is a complex interaction of initiatives called "Room for the River" designed to provide more space for the river and reduce flooding by relocating dykes, raising the dyke level, lowering the floodplains either side of the river, deepening the riverbed and removing obstacles. The location was the Netherlands, with cost of the Program at 2.4 billion Euro, and 39 Projects involved with the Initiation phase 2000-2006, followed by Design and Execution 2006 to 2015 (approximate).

This is a complex undertaking and most likely more difficult than anything that most of us will be involved in, however some important principles apply especially about balancing between potentially competing priorities. (This often occurs in large organizations where individual parts (departments, divisions, functions etc.) are required to collaborate in an overall program of work at an organizational level).

Some important lessons identified by the authors of the case are:

- Programs need to acknowledge the complexity of the context in which they operate;

- Effective stakeholder engagement at all levels can reconcile competing interests between national and local regions (or corporate and divisions). Plans and designs of the 39 projects were developed by the project teams in collaboration with the stakeholders of the local context;

- A centralized program office or program management function that is able to respond to uncertain and changing conditions is important. They can monitor progress, quality of plans and achievement of objectives based on a philosophy of "controlled trust". This is created by transparency of roles and responsibilities between local and central levels during the various stages of each of the projects in the program. Continual alignment and adaption is required;

- Central program office / program management function can enhance capacity of project teams through training sessions and acting as a conduit between local and centralized stakeholders. They can facilitate projects by providing guidelines for issues common across projects.

- The program office and project teams had a combined focus on strategy and performance. Traditionally projects focus on performance and programs on strategy however the combination here in the case study facilitated a collaborative approach;

- Standard project structures and roles were applied which enhanced knowledge sharing and learning across the projects and amongst the individuals involved across various organizations and between the various levels of government.

- Plans and designs of the 39 projects were developed by the project teams in collaboration with the stakeholders of the local context.

These principles can be adapted and utilized to ensure programs deliver the corporate vision while addressing local divisional or departmental needs. Achieving effective collaboration among business units is a challenge for many organizations and very critical for successful program management.

Systems Thinking

I have constantly throughout this book made reference to taking a systems view in order to understand the larger picture that produces business value and not to divide it into components and try and manage at that level. Some may say that systems thinking approaches may be a dilemma since it is not a natural and comfortable approach for many managers. Alistair Mant (1997) in his excellent book "Intelligent Leadership", tells the story of discussing inputs and outputs concepts using the television set in the classroom with a group of 7-year-old children. After some discussion they were able to develop a concept like the picture below, which confirmed for him that we have a natural instinct for thinking in this fashion, which then is probably diminished through the traditional education system, which tends to isolate learning into discrete siloed activities. This point about education has also been raised by other writers in various forums.

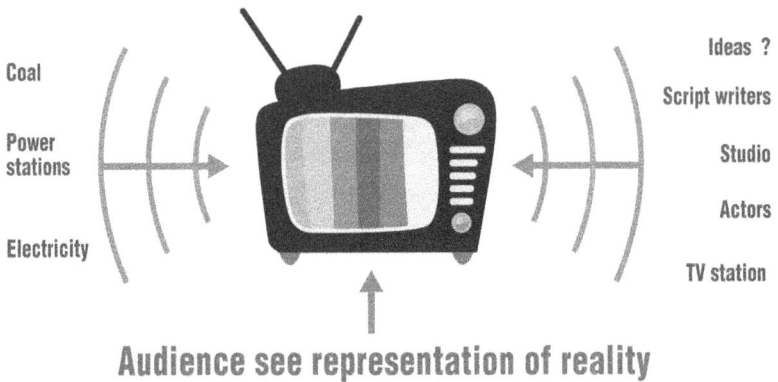

Audience see representation of reality

Figure 15 - Example of Systems Thinking in Practice

I believe it is quite possible through various means to encourage and assist managers and staff at all levels in the organization to think more clearly about systems rather than just piecemeal activities. This is important in order to obtain positive results since there are too many instances of initiatives creating unintended consequences due to limited understanding of the total system in which they are making change. The mapping techniques referred to in Chapter 4 is one approach to enhancing systems thinking.

(See Resources for more information on Systems Thinking and potential sources.)

Steps to Migrate to or Advance to Program Management

Having considered the challenges to implementing Program Management may I suggest some ideas about steps you might take?

The steps depend heavily on the context but some ideas are:

- Ensure there are clear strategic level drivers for this change to program management which relate to improving the value from the organizations investment in strategy implementation. There will be opposition as it will be seen as another overhead.

- Analysis of the current effectiveness of strategy implementation and the value derived from it. Conducting several Post–Implementation–Reviews on past projects to implement strategy will provide some useful insights. If there has been a significant failure to implement strategy an independent analysis of the reasons should provide useful background context.

- Commitment from the highest level of management in the organization is necessary, ideally at a Board level. Create awareness across the organization and particularly in the business units about the different approach of the program management. You may need an external facilitator to assist with this. Migrating to program management is a business change initiative and should be treated in that way.

- Review the organizations KPIs to ensure that managers have an incentive to carefully implement strategy to achieve the planned value, and not just be concerned about the business as usual activity of their own business units.

- Select a candidate initiative, which should be a strategy or a part thereof. Specify how it will be managed differently to a project.

- Either recruit or contract an experienced program manager to assist in setting it up. Appoint one of your business managers to shadow the program manager and learn how to manage the program. It may be possible after some duration (say 6 or more months) for the business manager who is shadowing to take over from the program manager who can then play a coaching and supporting role.

- After 12 months do a lessons learned review. What worked well, what did not work well, and is there still support for this new approach

Reflection

As a management practice Program Management is less defined and clear-cut than project management and may be less attractive to some managers who are looking for more certainty. Program management is realistic about strategic level issues because it recognizes the ambiguity and fuzziness and inherent messiness at this level (see quote at start of this Chapter) and seeks to work around it using the approach outlined in this book. However it still uses project management to deliver components and capability once we know and understand what we are seeking to achieve in terms of organizational benefits.

At all times overall organizational value (and not that of individual silos) is the ultimate key driver and focus for our program endeavors.

Endnotes

- Mant, Alistair (1997) *"Intelligent leadership"*, Allen &Unwin, St. Leonards, Australia
- Mitroff, Ian I & Lindstone Harold A, (1993), *The Unbounded Mind Breaking the Chains of Traditional Business Thinking"* Oxford university Press, NY
- Rijke, J van Herk, S Zevenbergen, C Ashley, R   Hertogh, M ten Heuvelhof, E (2014) "Adaptive programme management through a balanced performance / strategy oriented focus", *International Journal of Project Management,* 32, 1197-1209
- Sull, D Homkes, R & Sull, C (2015) "Why Strategy Execution Unravels – and what to do about it", *Harvard Business Review,* March
- Ward, John et al (2013*), "Beating the odds – the secrets of successful programmes",* International Centre for Programme Management at Cranfield – see Resources at end for link to the paper

RESOURCES

<u>References to Standards</u>

- PMI, (2013) The Standard for Program Management, Project Management Institute, 3rd Edn, Newtown Square, Penn, USA www.pmi.org
- Cabinet Office, UK Government (2011) *Managing Successful Programs,* The Stationery Office, Norwich - now available from https://www.axelos.com/
- P2M - A Guidebook of Project and Program Management for Enterprise Innovation – Project Management Association of Japan - Available from: http://www.pmaj.or.jp/ENG/index.htm
- APM (2007) APM Introduction to Programme Management, available to purchase from https://www.apm.org.uk/IntroToPM

<u>Other Resources</u>

- International Centre for Program Management – Cranfield University has some useful papers on the topic but you will need to search for them: http://www.som.cranfield.ac.uk/som/p16914/knowledge-interchange/management-themes/programme-and-project-management
  (note the papers have moved recently and this is best link as at 1st January 2017)
- GAPPS (2011) A framework for performance based competency standards for Program Managers – available from: http://www.globalpmstandards.org/main/page_home.html
- Thiry, Michel (2010) Program Management, Gower, Farnham Surrey

Systems Thinking – Understanding Systems – Resources

Throughout the book I have been emphasizing the need for programs to understand the system in which they operate in order to be able to produce the desired outcomes. I have particularly referred to this in Chapter 5 "Challenges in Implementing Program Management", and noted that it is not too difficult to educate managers to think this way, although I do acknowledge that organizational culture, practices and procedures can get in the way of achieving this.

There are several resources that I have referred to in the book that will aid your understanding.

- Dörner, Dietrich (1996). *"The Logic of Failure – recognising and avoiding error in complex situations"*, Basic books, New York
- Senge, Peter (1990) *The Fifth Discipline*, Random House, New York
- Dettmer, H W (1998) *Breaking the Constraints to World-Class Performance*, ASQ Quality Press, Wisconsin

Also I would like to add another resource from which I have extracted the following summary material.

- *Meadows, Donella & (Editor) Wright, Diana, 2008 "Thinking in Systems – A primer"*, Sustainability Institute, Chelsea Green Publishing , Vermont USA

Summary of Systems Principles

Systems:

- a system is more than the sum of its parts;
- many of the interconnections in systems operate through the flow of information;

- the least obvious part of the system, its function or purpose, is often the most crucial determinant of the system's behavior;

- system structure is the source of systems behavior. Systems behavior reveals itself as a series of events over time.

Where to draw the boundary around the system depends on the purpose of the discussion.

The bounded rationality of each actor (i.e. making decisions within their limited understanding or framework) in the system may not lead to decisions that serve the welfare of the system as a whole.

Also here are some quotes worth remembering –taken from "Think Twice: Harnessing the Power of Counter-intuition" by Michael J. Mauboussin, Harvard Business Press, 2009, Boston

"Humans have a deep desire to understand cause and effect, as such links probably conferred humans with evolutionary advantage. In complex adaptive systems, there is no simple method for understanding the whole by studying the parts, so searching for simple agent-level causes of system-level effects is useless. Yet our minds are not beyond making up a cause to relieve the itch of an unexplained effect. When a mind seeking links between cause and effect meets a system that conceals them, accidents will happen."

"So if you deal with a complex adaptive system, make sure you carefully set your system-level goal and proceed with caution in implementing agent-level changes for achieving your objective."

Today organizations are typically complex adaptive systems. Programs are also mostly designed to make changes to these complex adaptive systems. Therefore you need to be able to understand the system overall and not be too buried in the detail where the "agent-level" causes, to use his term, operate. We see many instances of organizations taking action to fix the symptoms of the problem rather than the root cause and this typically makes the problem worse, or causes unintended consequences that cannot be foreseen. So Michael's quotes caution us to beware of doing this and focus on the overall system.

Our mental models guide our understanding of the system and we may need to change them. Peter Senge in his book The Fifth Discipline mentioned above talks about mental models. What are your mental models? How do they influence your understanding of the world?

Author

Harold Ainsworth has held senior management positions in several project service organizations involving oversight of large complex projects, and been responsible for several organization change management initiatives. Also he has considerable experience as a consultant and educator in portfolio, program and project management in both Australia and South East Asia. His current consulting work is in helping organizations achieve sustainable value from their strategic investments through effective Governance, and the practices of portfolio, program and project management.

Harold holds post-graduate qualifications in management and is a member of four professional organizations, and he teaches part-time at two Australian Universities in their graduate Project Management Programs.

"Harold's ability to translate complex matters into consumable information is again borne out in this book. As the author makes abundantly clear, distinguishing between a project and program is a primary lesson that, when applied, will generate tangible business outcomes and benefit. Programs are where the real business benefits come from."
- Ms. Genéne Kleppe, Executive Director, GKforge – Designing for the Future

www.ingramcontent.com/pod-product-compliance
Lightning Source LLC
Chambersburg PA
CBHW071115210326
41519CB00020B/6310